EMBERS UNDER MY SKIN

Poems and Photos

by Albert Russo

EMBERS UNDER MY SKIN - Poems and Photos by Albert Russo

Copyright © 2012 Albert Russo

All rights reserved.

ISBN-13: 978-1-935437-56-7 (paperback)
ISBN-10: 1-935437-56-9 (paperback)

Published in the United States of America by
IMAGO PRESS - 3710 East Edison - Tuczon, AZ 85716

Some of these poems have appeared in:
Reach, Aquillrelle (UK), The Taj Mahal Review and Labyrinth (India),
Editions Labor, Los Muestros and Voix du Congo (Belgium) and
The Pedestal magazine (USA), garnering several awards from The Writer's Digest (USA).

Author's website: www.albertrusso.eu

EMBERS UNDER MY SKIN - Poems and Photos by Albert Russo

OFFERING TO MY FELLOW POETS	6
CREATIVE MOODS	8
ECHOES OF THE FLESH	12
LOST IDENTITY	14
THE WEIGHT OF THINGS	16
LOVE TENUOUS	18
AMOR LATINO	20
MAN OH MAN!	22
THE STAGES OF LOVE	26
HISTORY AS JUST ANOTHER BAD DREAM	30
THE ROSE CITY OF PETRA	36
EILAT OF CORAL	40
A DAY IN OUR LIVES	44
A LIFE STORY	48
LE BEL KONGO	52
THE GHOSTS OF THE BELGIAN CONGO	58
A WIDE WILD WHITE WORLD	62
YOU SHALL MARK MY WORDS	66
SEVEN BILLION MIRACLES	74
SO SMALL, SO VITAL	76
THE SEED THAT GREW	80
EMBELLISHED YOUTH	88
WHO MADE US THE WAY WE ARE?	94
ALIENATED	102
THE FATE OF A BRILLIANT YOUNG MIND	106
MISSED APPOINTMENT	110
IN THE GARDENS OF VILLA BORGHESE	114
THE BEAUTY OF SYMMETRY	118
Biography, reviews and more photos	120

Some of these poems have appeared in: Aquillrelle (UK), The Taj Mahal Review and Labyrinth (India), Editions Labor, Los Muestros and Voix du Congo (Belgium), garnering several awards from The Writer's Digest (USA).
Author's website: www.albertrusso.eu

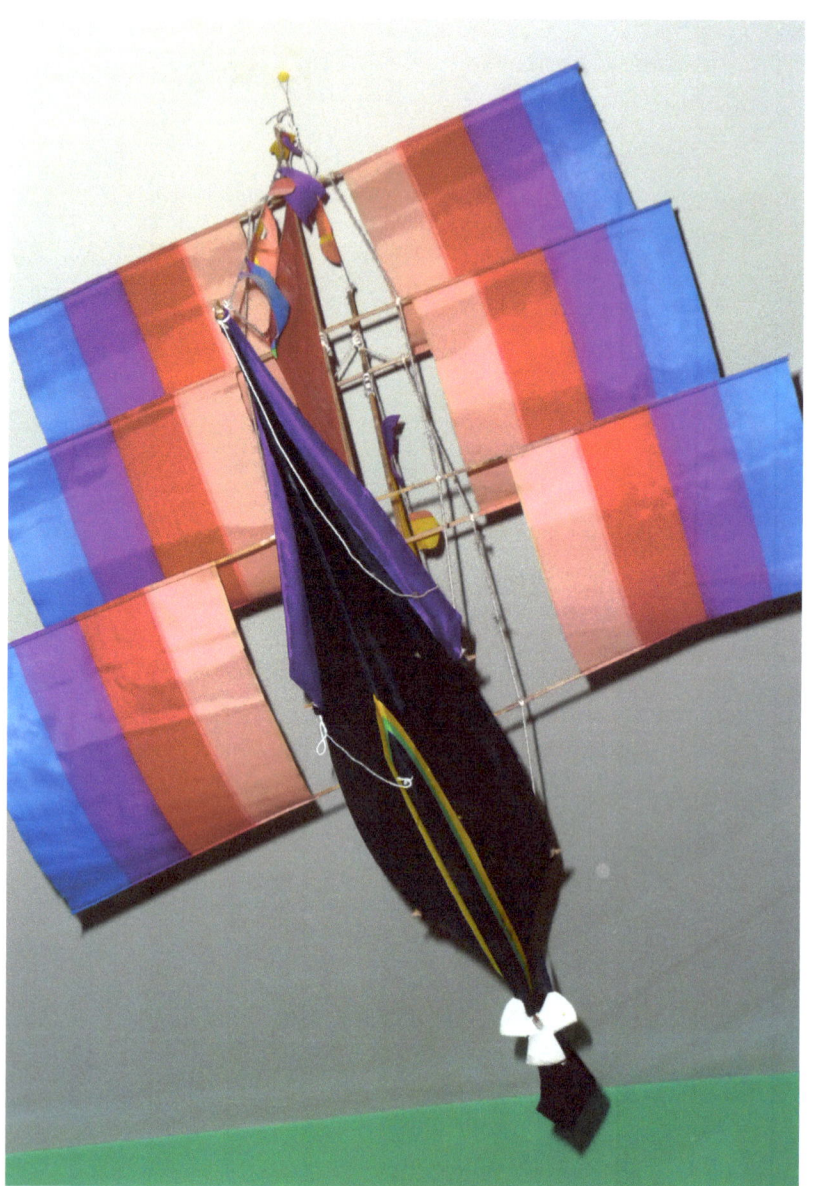

OFFERING TO MY FELLOW POETS

a scathing review
should not cast you in a trance
though your blood cries out

are you stuck with words?
then string them
around your neck
they will set you free

whatever they say
remember Kipling's advice
about self-control

a drop of honey
a taste of eternity
wrapped in syllables

thanks to the haiku
you can recreate the world
or leave not a trace

before man could speak
he knew poetry
by intuition

diplomacy
is the language one uses
when love has no place

like ships in the night
like clouds shredding in the blue
like your closing heart

the boat is sinking
but who thinks of the havoc
wrought in the ocean

travel to the stars
with your bag of memories
and earth's illusions

in desperation
let dreams carry you away
they'll color your pain

CREATIVE MOODS

the act of writing
is like a plunge in the void
or a muffled sigh

when you're inspired
it is smooth as a pebble
swept by clear water

a storm breaks out
in the middle of the sentence
and the world is a blur

the room reeks of death
the stench is unbearable
rust-colored ink

it's been so long since
my fingers held a pen
they feel arthritic

screen and computer
have replaced dad's Underwood
I hear his heartbeats

too much idleness
numbs the imagination
wind of a glacier

ECHOES OF THE FLESH

Do you hear that sound
the clicking in your entrails
like the distant rumble of war?
Picture the battles being waged
inside your body
the blood cells colliding
in the midst of a snow storm
Is it Napoleon's troops
falling like pegs
at the gates of Moscow
or the last German battalions
being decimated
in the deadliest of
a Russian winter?
The echo grows louder
until it fills every inch
of your bones
You try to move a leg
a gesture repeated
a million times by rote
but suddenly your limbs
refuse to obey
history has a way
of taking its revenge
some call it karma

LOST IDENTITY

tell me what to do
tell me where to go
am I losing my bearings?
Why are you still by my side?
I don't recognize you anymore
I can't remember the good times
they seem to have dissolved
into a slipstream
give me your hand
I want to feel its pulse
I'm suddenly so cold inside
and terribly spare
because it is not you
I've become a stranger to
but myself

THE WEIGHT OF THINGS

How much can one endure?
What amount of pain
can a person take
before s/he collapses?
see the little girl
whose heart broke
as she watched her ragdoll
fall into the lake
or the street urchin
who swore he would never
go back home after
the last beating
his drunken father gave him
remember the haggard looks
on those emaciated faces
behind the barbed wire
of a concentration camp
or Marilyn Monroe
shrieking in the middle
of the desert, in 'The Misfits'
when one of the men
began lassoing a mustang
with all his might
how much can one endure,
yes, how much?

LOVE TENUOUS

I hate to see myself
being hurt by his careless quips
and in turn having to retaliate
which I do, unwillingly

sorry, he moans, so sorry
I really didn't mean it
you know how I blurt out things
I just can't help myself sometimes
but you also know
how much you count for me
WITHOUT YOU I am NOTHING

those words make you
bleed inside
bleed to the point of
becoming blind to his new pain,
self-inflicted, and well deserved, you insist

he then rests his hand
on your shoulder
but you push it violently aside
afraid that one more of his quips
will dampen your love forever

AMOR LATINO
Variations

Amour fou
amour à mort
ti amo per l'eternità
amor y mas amor
la passion
le désamour
la haine
c'est la guerre
passato l'amore
non conta più nulla
sin amor
la vida no es vida
fragore dell'amore
senza respiro
meglio suicidarsi
chè morire
senza amore
fini l'amour
mort pour de bon
AMOR, il nome di ROMA,
Rome, la ville éternelle
car toujours
l'amour s'y renouvelle

MAN, OH MAN!

If you could just say hello to
your neighbor, this stranger
so different from you,
in color and in creed.
Black is beautiful indeed,
this is no mere slogan,
for Africa, after all, is
the cradle of our one
and only race
if you could outline a smile
when she passes by
instead of always pretending
you are in a hurry
if you could lend her a hand
when she drops
her errands on the pavement
you would make two people happy,
my fellow man
no, I wouldn't call you a friend,
not just yet
and the birds would start
trilling joyously over our heads
If instead of always blaming others
for your sorry plight
and for all the ills of this world

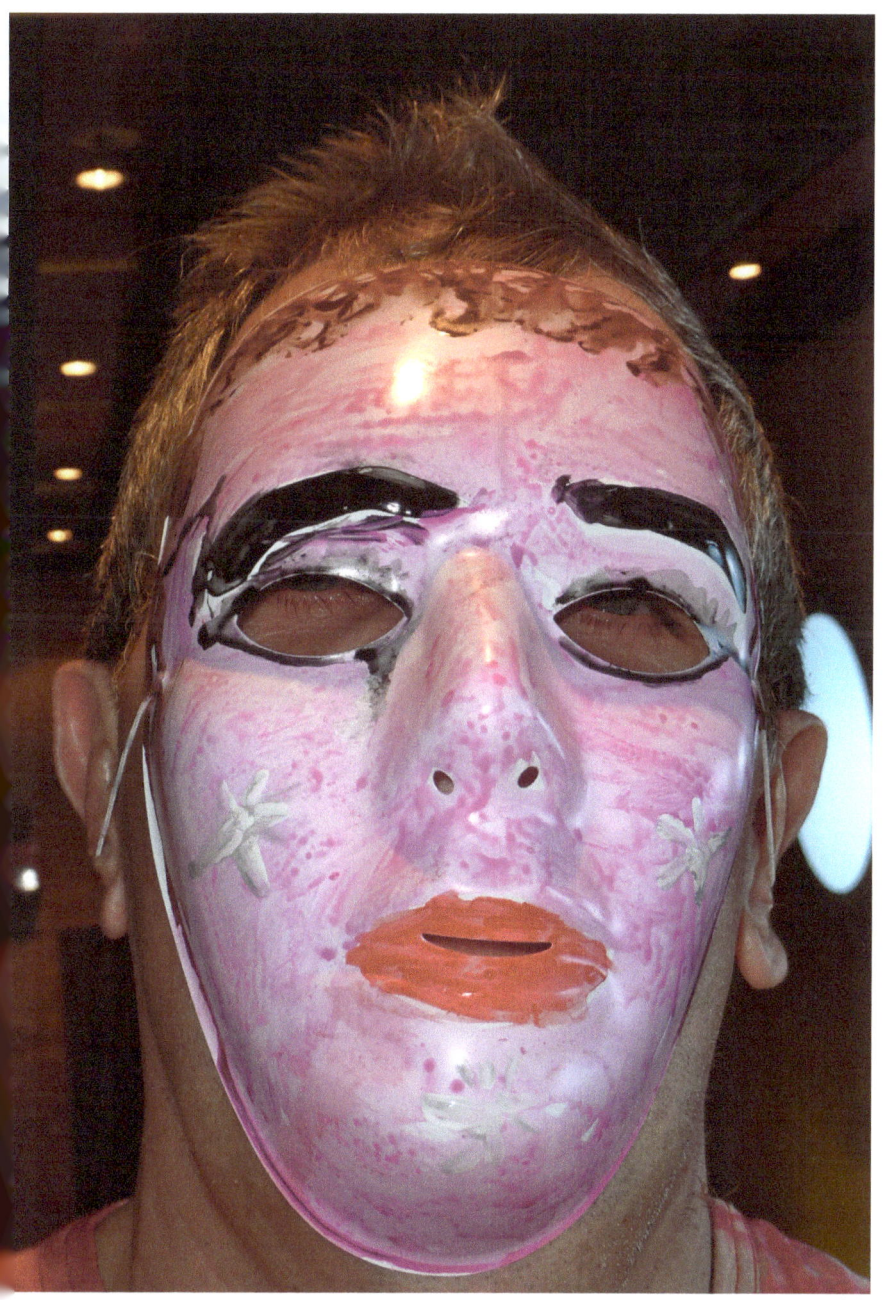

you would try to emulate
the industrious folk of
China and of India,
of South Korea and of Japan,
the most ancient cultures
of our planet,
who use their intelligence
and their energy
to build a brighter future
for their children.
If you could only treat
Woman as your equal,
and stop wishing she were
at your disposal,
short of being your slave,
considering sex
as dirty and sinful,
a mere tool for the act
of procreation,
which explains your
secular frustration
and your ensuing crimes,
mysogenous, homophobic
and otherwise
Then and only then,
you might reintegrate
the human community
of the Heart

THE STAGES OF LOVE

diaphanous blue
cloven by the Eiffel Tower
in your virgin space

a veil of dust
draping my body
the sound of your breath

Velo di polvere
Vestendo il mio corpo
il tuo respiro

iridescent dot
sucked into a chalice
flower tongues ladybug

the moment your lips meet
you can kiss friendship goodbye
the flesh takes over

bocca a bocca
non è più amicizia
la carne vince

skin against skin
and the magic operates
till the cells rebel

the difference between
a sex maniac and a lover
body temperature

la differenza tra
maniaco ed amante
il tocco

beware dear lovers
passion is a clash of wills
bound to implode

he fell in love with her,
but she looked elsewhere, smitten,
his heart a gaping wound

s'innamoro di lei
senza rendersi conto
solitudine

HISTORY AS JUST ANOTHER BAD DREAM

When you lose
a fellowman in Darfur
and see your sister being raped
by a horde of Jenjaweed
and have to lie down, soaked
in the blood of your neighbor,
pretending you are dead

When you remember the scene
of crushed skulls, buzzing
with green flies
in the hills of Rwanda
a few years ago

When you wake up in a sweat
reliving Pol Pot's
mass killings in Cambodia

When was that again,
during the twentieth century,
1870, 1070, or the year 70?

When the hell did
all of this happen?
does it really truly matter?

you wonder whether the fact
that you are still alive
is another quirky twist of fate.
Listen to that homunculus
asserting that
the holocaust is a hoax,
promising that he will wipe out
the State of Israel.

Listen to those neo-nazis
in Russia and in America
for whom black is still and always the color of doom
and gypsies ought to be sent back to the gas chambers
along with the gays and,
who else, the Jews, of course.

Listen to Radio Maria and
its archbishop, Arch-antisemite,
blaming everything on the 'Yids', when Poland,
which numbered 3.5 million of them before World War II
has only Auschwitz left
to remind him of their past existence
it is now their ghosts
he cannot suffer,
he who purports to represent Christ on earth
and who idolizes the Virgin Mary,
both terribly terribly Jewish.

And what about
the five million Congolese
who died of famine, of disease
of torture; during the last decade?
Yes, what about them?
Where the hell are the reporters?

Selective memory seems to be
the curse of the day,
and who ever said History
has come to an end?

It is the reflection of our darkest soul
and we want to bury it along
with all the Auschwitzes
we have erected,
so that we can build new ones
without remorse.

THE ROSE CITY OF PETRA

Behind the mount of Hor
where Aaron is buried
in the Valley of Moses
the Nabateans
built palaces of splendor
carved in the rock
lofty canyons scraping
the sky of a limpid
translucent blue
Surrounded by the desert
a thousand walls
sprout in phantasmal hues
from sand pink to coal brown
through all the shades of coral
defying the laws of gravity
Walking in the narrow corridors
that separate them
you feel at once dwarfed
and exhilirated
imagining you are
the emissary of a foreign court
awaited by the King of Petra
And the towering walls
stand guard, protecting you
all the way to the palace

Then all of a sudden
as if emerging from a dream
between the cracks of a gorge
a doric column appears
holding parts of
a monumental crown
An ethereal silence sets in
and you slow your pace
lest the miracle fades
into a mirage
the air is brimming with
sand particles
yet you fear that
if you remain still
you will be turned into
a pillar of salt
like Lot's wife in the Bible
your feet shuffle on
the pebbly ground
and the crunching sound
fills you with terror
then in a surge of courage
you slip out of the crack
and face the majestic facade
of the golden Khaznah

EILAT OF CORAL

Dakota standing guard
at the tip of the runway
shining jet takes off

White and blue DC3
a pioneer of Israel
the desert all around

Sun sets over Eilat
brocade in pink and violet
The Red Sea switches off

Lofty palm trees
congregate on the boardwalk
bowing to the sky

Amid the handsome youth
old bones creak
under the weight
of past tragedies

Faces of all hues

they hail from Ethiopia
and the Russian steppes
from Melbourne
and Montevideo
from Quebec
and Cape Town

They laugh
and walk
in droves

or follow shadows
carrying their solitude

Mirror of
the world

A DAY IN OUR LIVES

Children playing in the courtyard
little Steven throws a ball at Laura
she gets it on the face and yells
the boy is scared and runs away
her friend takes her in her arms
then wipes the blood
from her nose

the dog lies on the porch,
it is resting
the family cat comes
and licks its muzzle
the dog groans contentedly
but doesn't move
in the livingroom a parrot shrieks
"what's all the schmoozing about?"

a lonely ant scampers
along a crack in the floor
a man's shoe tries to crush it
in vain
spiteful, he says:
"there are billions of them
and I couldn't get this one."

the ant retorts: "like you
I'm an individual,
so, respect my life,
as I respect yours"

far, far away, thousands
of miles from here
a suicide bomber destroys
the lives of 110 human beings

yet, in her dream, she was sure
it happened right next door
the moment she wakes up,
the TV is on,
showing her the disastrous effect
of that attack

whether you want it or not,
you're always in harm's way

a bird chirps merrily
behind the rosebush
as if this planet resembled
the paradise Adam could admire
on the sixth day
of God's Creation

A LIFE STORY

when you're in a daze
not sure whether you're awake
or still dreaming
you will yourself
from the farthest memories
to unfurl your life

then, overwhelmed
you catch yourself embracing
every single detail

your first steps as a child
yesterday's road accident
your grandfather's smile

it's all helter-skelter
yet, so truelike, so vivid
so physical

remember that song?
swimming in Lake Tanganyika
the wailing refugees

spring in New York
chopped chicken liver on rye
you're still a freshman

look at your hands
yes, the years have passed
but your heart hasn't aged

indeed, you insist
as if to defy time
I am all those things

the past

the present

and the future

LE BEL KONGO
rêve récurrent

C'est un pays qui m'a vu naître
au plus profond de l'humanité africaine
un pays où j'ai vécu une illusion du paradis
un pays où le Blanc se croyait si supérieur,
qu'il restait aveugle aux immenses qualités
de ces Congolais sans qui rien n'aurait pu se construire

Ensemble, ils avaient pourtant réalisé des merveilles:
Le chemin de fer, des milliers de kilomètres de rail
à travers la brousse et la forêt,
un superbe réseau fluvial,
un service sanitaire sans pareil sur le continent,
et dont toute la population bénéficiait,
quelle que fût sa couleur,
éradiquant ainsi toutes ces maladies tropicales
qui depuis l'Indépendance ont
malheureusement réapparu

Mais tout cela s'accomplissait
dans la séparation, l'apartheid

Si je pouvais me doter de pouvoirs divins
je réécrirais l'histoire de ce pays tant aimé
reprenant les choses au temps de
Stanley l'explorateur,
avant que Léopold II, ce roi félon, ne se mette à saigner
cet immense territoire qu'il considérait comme
son jardin privé,
sous prétexte d'avoir éliminé l'esclavage
que les Arabes professaient impunément
depuis des siècles dans la région,
il utilisa ces mêmes hommes pour l'extraction
du caoutchouc et de l'ivoire,
les soumettant à un labeur inhumain
Ce scandale fut bientôt décrié
par les autres puissances coloniales,
très hypocritement,
convaincues qu'elles étaient au début
que le Congo n'était qu'un enfer vert
d'où rien d'utile ne surgirait

J'ai cependant goûté dans ce merveilleux pays
aux joies et aux peines de ses habitants
ces peuples autochtones, qu'ils soient du Kasaï,
du Kivu, du Katanga ou de l'Equateur,
me recevaient toujours avec une gentillesse
et une générosité dont beaucoup
d'Occidentaux en Europe font défaut.

J'ai eu cette chance de vivre
la fin de la colonisation,
où l'espoir se dessinait sur les lèvres
de nos frères noirs

Temps d'arrêt : avec les si,
nous referions le monde,

Mais personne
ne m'empêchera de continuer
à rêver de ce qui aurait pu
et pourrait encore être:
un pays démocratique,
nommé le Bel Kongo
où tous vivraient
dans le respect
et l'harmonie.

THE GHOSTS OF
THE BELGIAN CONGO

When, during a balmy
autumn evening,
I stroll along the avenues
of Brussels' southern outskirts
not so far from the plains
that surround Waterloo,
where the English dealt
a fatal blow
to Napoleon's dream
of a French Europe

my eyes take in each one
of those opulent homes,
Tudor or Art Nouveau,
Third Empire or Bauhaus,
Flemish, or in the lofty style
of the fifties,
as if, in a previous
or imagined life,
I had inhabited them all
at one period or another
and I get the eerie impression
that a ghost lurks
behind some leafy tree
that it will sneak
out of a mansion,

burning to meet me
and whisper something
I already know,
for it always happens thus,
when, after a distance of years,
I return to these parts,
the presence of such ghosts
is indeed soothing to me
for they have spanned
the decades, plied the seas
and the deserts
to bring news from the land
of my youth, Zaire,
which was once the Belgian Congo
there's a subtle, mysterious bond
that ties a former colonial power
to its erstwhile colony
in spite of the vicissitudes
and the painful divorce,
a bond harbored in
these tranquil homes
as in old bones
which neither time nor latitude
will ever erase, not even
the faint traffic rumble
of Europe's capital,
which suddenly reminds me,
dinner must be ready

A WILD WHITE WORLD

I woke up lying on a beach
it was a sparkling stretch of sand
soft and warm, under my body
I should have felt elated
but, strangely, neither joy
nor gloom affected me
Before my eyes spread
a wide expanse of water,
great, lofty waves,
splashing the air
with the muffled echo
of a myriad crackers
it was the color of milk
the horizon was surrounded
by mountains
and the peaks were capped
with fresh snow
here again, the range stood
draped in a whitish gauze
far behind me
I could perceive
a mangrove
that too was doused in white

now and then the maddening buzz
of mosquitoes would invade my head
Feeling my pulse, I started to panic
my limbs shimmered
as if covered with cocaine powder
White ought to be the reflection of light
the favorite shade of brides
the color of all things
lovely and pure
but this whiteness
was like nothing on earth
Might we then be standing
on the threshold of the Garden of Eden
in which, so claim the suicide bombers,
Allah's promises will materialize
with virgins galore, for those 'brave men'
who kill dozens of infidels,
That there are innocent
children and invalids
among them is but a mere detail
How about the woman folk,
what do they get for their 'sacrifice'?
do they just stare at their
'martyr' brothers and husbands
and serve them savory tidbits
and Turkish delights,
while they make love to the nymphs?

YOU SHALL MARK MY WORDS

I, Yeshua ben Yosef, son of our beloved Myriam,
turn to you who have forsaken and betrayed me,
you who claim to be such good Christians,
all the while you have tried to erase the Jew in me,
you have done that on every continent,
and many of you are still doing it, unashamedly,
out of habit or out of sheer ignorance,
for, let it be known, now and forever :
the enemy of my People is my enemy

2000 years have passed before a pope
has asked for forgiveness
It is never too late, you will say
it may not be too late for your children
or for the generations to come,
but it is far too late for the countless
brothers and sisters
who were chased, tortured and murdered
by the Spanish and Portuguese Inquisitors
it is far too late for the tens of thousands of
brothers and sisters
who were persecuted and killed
during the Russian and the Polish pogroms

it is far too late for all those millions of
brothers and sisters
who were treated like animals,
tormented then gassed
by the nazis, who perpetrated
history's most diabolic crime
as it is much too late for
the numerous refugees whom
the Allies turned away during WWII,
as they desperately
sought a haven on their shores

Was then Jewish life, as a French fascist still insists today,
just a mere detail, too negligible to consider?
It appeared so

I have always maintained that I was the son of man,
as is every Jew who is made in the image of his Creator
Yet, you have declared that I was the Son of God
in reality, I was a simple man who loved his neighbor
as much as he despised the profiteers and the hypocrites,
and like a rabbi, I would praise the Lord on Shabbat
at the synagogue, the synagogue which
you converted into a church,
though it had never been my intention to
transform the House of God,
a man who celebrated the holy days
of Pessah, of Rosh Ashana and of Kippur,
the definitions of which you should go and relearn

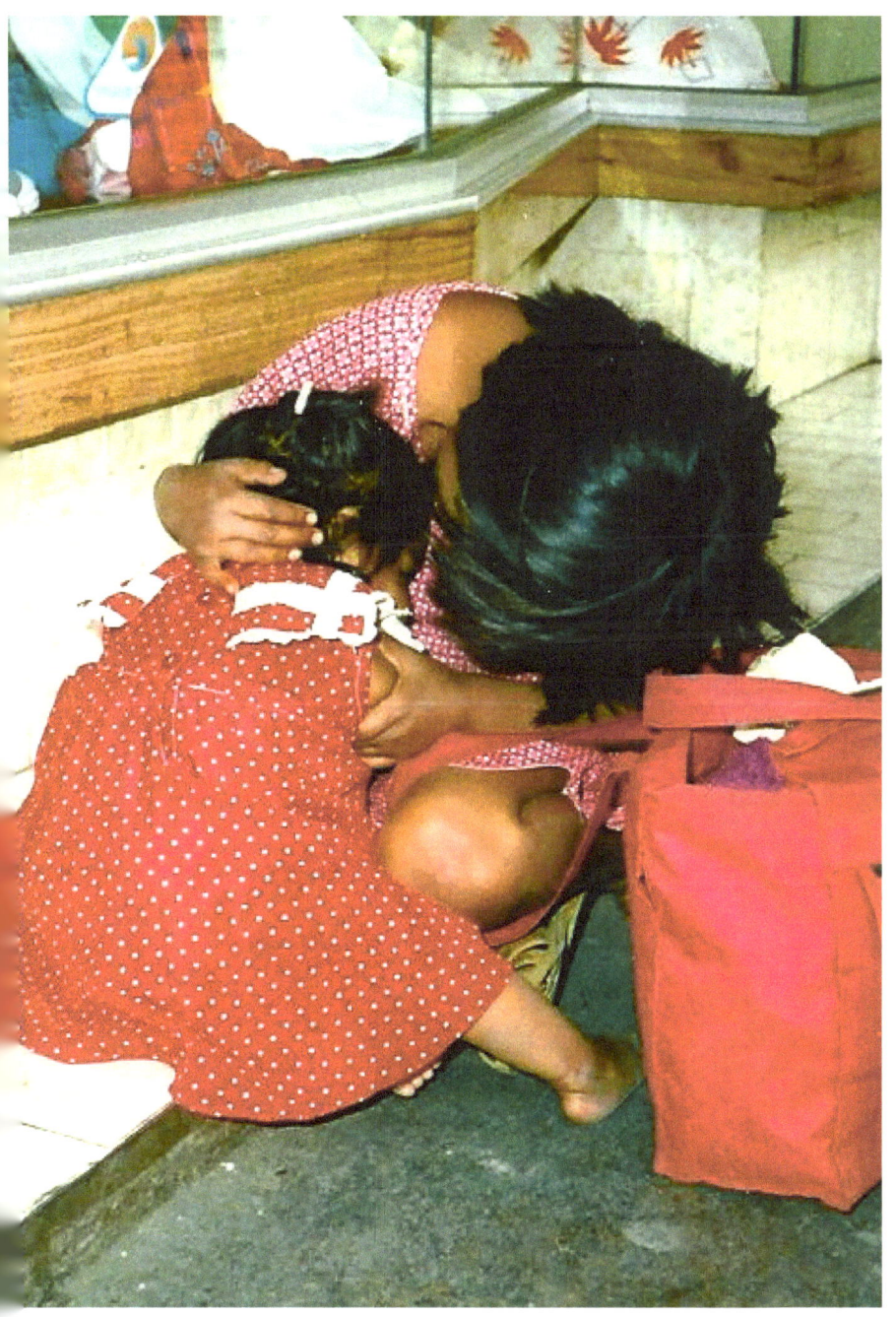

*So few of you remember what
the Christian New Year means:
the date of my circumcision,
which like all Jewish baby boys
is performed eight days after birth
Christmas, in my case
Had I, as your messiah, returned to earth
between 1940 and 1945,
I would have been sent directly to
a nazi concentration camp,
after the humiliating stripping of my clothes and
the exhibition of my manhood;
would you or the pope have recognized me then,
amid the horrors of war?
It was the Romans who crucified me
yet you persisted in accusing my People
as if humans could actually kill God!*

*Call me by my name, which, I repeat, is Yeshua,
a name you have translated into Jesus,
like the Torah, which is at the root and heart of
Christian civilization,
if that is an old testament, then what are the Gospels
supposed to be? A confabulation, a plagiary?
'Traduttore', traditore, as the Italian saying goes,
like all the words you have put in my mouth,
distorting some of them from their original meaning*

I shall forgive you, poor sinners,
yes, I shall forgive you,
the day you will love me in all sincerity,
the day you will love my People
as much as yourselves
Remember the Just, who, throughout the centuries -
they were the best of Christians, of Muslims,
of Hindus and of Buddhists,
the best of animists, of agnostics and of atheists,
indeed they were
my blood brothers and my blood sisters -,
so often risked their own lives
to save their Jewish neighbors
from the claws of their torturers,
they acted out of love,
out of compassion, for every human being is made
in the image of his and her Creator,
with the free will to become good or evil,
just like Abel and Cain

SEVEN BILLION MIRACLES

a second has just slipped by
a needle in the haystack of Time
and while this line
is being couched
another second evaporates

blood pulses in your veins
the cells are in a constant turmoil
and the heart skips another beat
life flows like an undercurrent
whereas you are oblivious to it

each individual is
a miracle of creation
and yet, there are men, mostly men,
but a few women too, who want
to pit themselves against God
maiming and killing their fellowmen
in random terror attacks
and believe
those terrifying 'men-of-god'
who promise them
an afterlife of bliss
amid a harem of virgins

SO SMALL, SO VITAL
don't dismiss them like refuse
they're ingrained in you

Poem with a haiku title

Pretty coffeebean,
beckons the grain of rice,
don't look so despondent
you're not alone
remember, we're
humans' mainstay
without us most people would
look distraught or die of hunger
you tickle their buds
and pep them up
with your intoxicating aroma
whilst I challenge the imagination
of chefs around the world
who honor me in so many
delicious recipes

The arrogance,
counters the grain of salt,
what would humanity
do without us?
their food would be tasteless
and their life totally bleak
then too, if they abuse us

we have the power
to make them ill
even to shorten their lifeline
we command respect

Ho ho, butts in the grain of sand,
listen to these three
bragging about their fate
they get eaten and done with
whereas I live on, eternally
yes, forever and ever,
and humans fear us
or consider our multitude
with awe and admiration
for we can't be escaped
and every year that passes
our deserts expand
leaving them less space
to grow their food
and drying their wells

so who's the winner here?

All of you would
go down the drain
if I didn't exist,
murmurs the grain of hope
as a soft breeze
blows their way.

THE SEED THAT GREW

India has been on my mind
ever since I was a little boy
it all started in my grandfather's
small tailor shop on Manica road,
behind Salisbury's railway station
(Zimbabwe's capital is now
called Harare)
I loved to go and visit him
after school
for he often invited his
Hindu, Muslim and Christian friends
for a cup of tea

and they would discuss about
life, their families,
their jobs, philosophy and religion,
comparing the verses of
the Bible and of the Kuran,
commenting upon them,
often with such gusto,
that it sometimes grew into
shouting matches,
but those were always
benevolent exchanges
that ended with laughter
and blessings

I was too young to understand
the implication
of these heated debates
and I would soon leave
that joyful assembly
to amble along the street
where I would stop before
narrow storefronts
that were a jumble of
knick knacks and house tools,
with at times strings
of tiny bulbs alight
that gave you the impression
it was always Christmas
there were the inevitable
dead flies stranded in the corners
often amid these fascinating goodies
stood the alabaster model of the Taj Mahal
and that was when my imagination ran wild,
dreaming of maharajahs
and of princesses
one more beautiful than the other,
who wore jewels only the
Queen of England could match

Eventually I came to see
that most splendid of all mausoleums
with my own eyes
and cried I was so overwhelmed

then too, at the Ashoka hotel,
I caught a glimpse of
the most beautiful female specimen
of the human race
she was tall, haughty
and wore a golden sari
her hair tumbled down
almost to her waist
like a glinting cascade
her skin had the delicacy
of translucent porcelain
she disappeared like a vision
to the point that I still wonder
whether she was real

I was a teenager when
my family and I moved
to Bujumbura, in the
former Rwanda-Urundi
there, I attended
an 'interracial' school,
with European, African,
American, Indian and
Pakistani classmates

On Saturday afternoons,
I would go to the Asian quarter
to visit some of my new friends
whose folks always welcomed me
with great kindness, offering
homemade cookies and
freshly pressed juices
I would inhale the pungent smells
that came in from the kitchen
as if they were pure mountain air
then we would go to
the Kit Kat movie house
where I was introduced to
the Indian cinema
long long before Bollywood
would become known
and there too I watched
my first Soviet films,
Sadko and the cerulean
Kingdom of the Ocean,
the Brothers Karamazov

that is how India grew in my heart

EMBELLISHED YOUTH

When you were a child,
you were so shy
In town you didn't dare
greet your parent's friends
some people thought
you were impolite
When your mother sent you out
to do errands
you would often pretend
you lost the list
so that you wouldn't
go to the various stores
and make the required purchases
You were a good student,
a very good student
you almost always got
the top grades
but with such fear in the stomach
that it gave you nightmares
You were expected to be the best
people congratulated you
At the end of the year
when you walked down
the platform
laden with your
prizewinning trophies

Oh how you hated to hear
your name being called again
and again by the principal
with the repeated applause
you felt as though you were suddenly
stripped of all your clothes
in front of that roaring audience
which continued to
congratulate you
You had no friends and
disliked any kind of sport
the shoving and the bullying
of your classmates
You couldn't stand the jokes
they made about girls and sex
not so much because you were a prude
but because you deemed that
everybody deserved the same respect
actually you preferred
the company of girls
and were called a sissy
on account of it
Once you reached adolescence,
you began to wax poetic
whenever you mentioned
the picnics you spent with friends
in the splendid African landscape

you still remember with
a pinch of nostalgia
those flights over the Rift Valley,
Lake Tanganyika and Victoria Falls
You can still hear the rumblings
of the DC3 and the murmurs of the
Vickers Viscount

Strange how one arranges
one's memories as if playing god,
throwing fireworks over
a glum past
indeed, nostalgia is the frame
one tries to draw
around the chaotic pieces
of our lives
it dilutes the sadness
and the melancholy
We no longer wish to remember
and it helps to forget what
a bashful and miserable
little boy you were
the anxious teenager
people crossed in town

After all you, had a good life
but you didn't realize it

WHO MADE US THE WAY WE ARE?

Why do we always
magnify things
calling our planet beautiful?
What is so nice
about earthquakes
and tsunamis, about wildfires
and hurricanes,
about the Vesuvius
threatening millions of people?

It is almost natural, albeit horrific,
that humans kill other humans,
don't animals do the same?
Survival of the fittest, you will say,
but they do it without malice
whereas man tries to play god
he's jealous of the other species
whose gifts and qualities he lacks
he wants to fly, to swim underwater
to travel through the galaxies,
he bores deep into the ground
and blasts whole mountains
stealing from the earth and
from the oceans
to build new cities,
whilst the environment bleeds

*Overwhelmed by
his technological feats
he forgets that our planet
is our greatest, our only provider
no matter how erratic
or capricious
When you look at a cloudless sky
and embrace the iodized wind,
When you stop before
a budding rose
or listen to the splashing sounds
of the waves, your heart sings
When you hear the birds twitter
in the distance or smell
the warm perfume of a croissant
just out of the oven
your senses are blissfully aroused
and you want to kiss
the whole world
that world your peers continue
to desecrate, believing
they know best
what is good for you*

Whose fault is it if we
have been endowed
with the ability to think
and to invent
with ambitions that sometimes turn
into delusions of gandeur?

Is it not legitimate to wish
we were more polished?
Yes, whose fault is it that
we're made the way we are
so woefully imperfect?
if we therefore play at the lifelong,
life-threatening game
of hit or miss,
miss then hit and hit again?
Are we not the favorite toy
of a cruel, whimsical god
who turns us around like
an amusing puppet then
strikes vengefully as if
we were a punching ball?

he smothers us randomly, or en masse,
when he deems we deserve
collective punishment

whilst at the same time
we fight each other with the most vicious
and sophisticated weapons
until one day we shall
wipe out the human race

Who on earth killed the dinosaurs?
did we ever think that our planet
was the god we are talking
or wondering about
that planet of a myriad wonders
which inflicts upon us
countless miseries
and against which we rebel
with our tantrums

Are we not too complex
for our own good?
what does the single cell think?

Sleep, oh let me go to sleep
I'm so tired of being human,
of being burdened with
so many questions
that will forever remain
unanswered

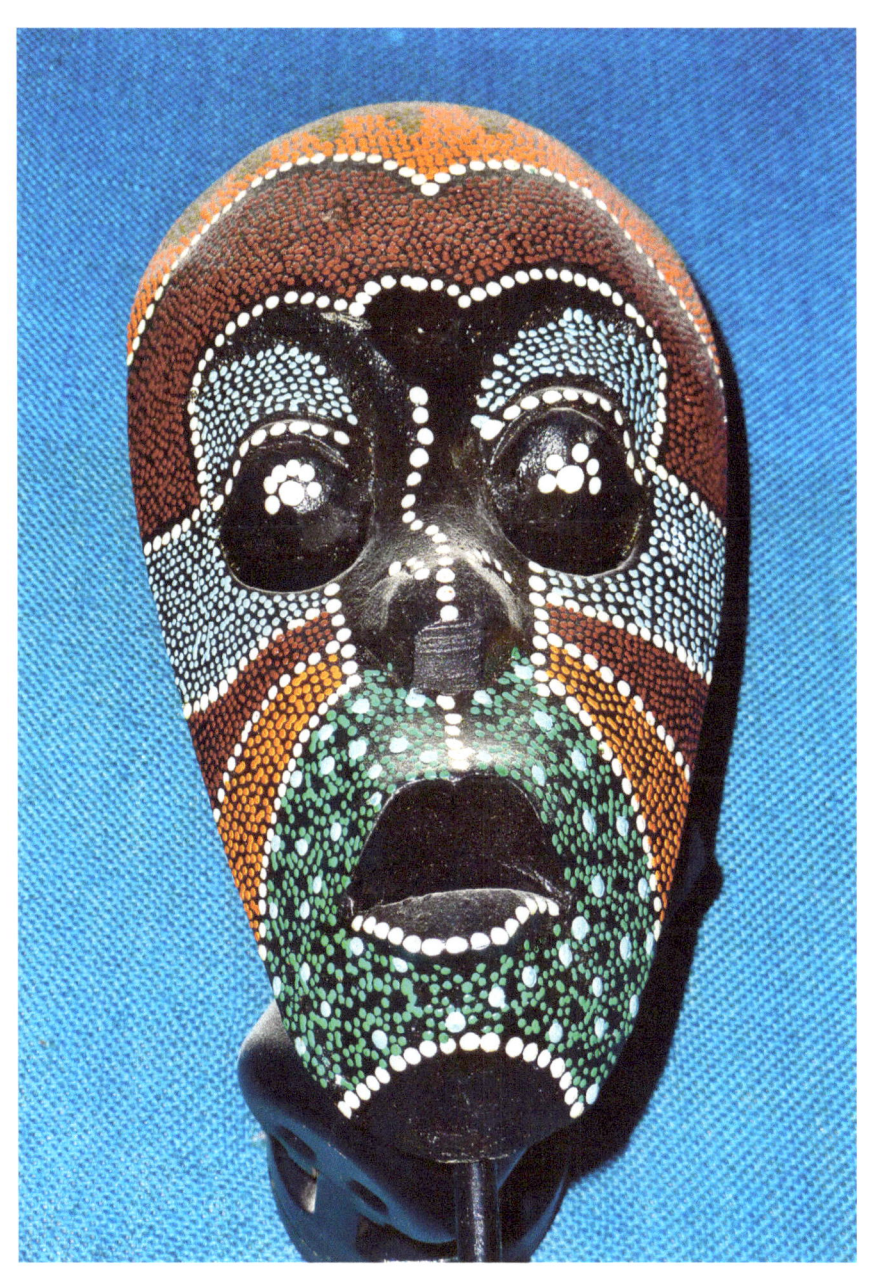

ALIENATED

he's lost his tongue
he can no longer verbalize
his lips drink the air

his nerves are frazzled
his heart is missing three beats
he swings between two worlds

his eyes are bleary
driving, he hoots in despair
he aims for the sideroad

he makes eye contact
she takes it as an insult
must he smile or run?

he holds the little boy's hand
and helps him cross the street
the mother panics

he orders smoked fish
it tastes like old meat
will he pay the bill?

he learns sign language
and reconnects with people
he's starting a new life

he discovers
the qualities of silence
less becomes more

he meets her in the park
their gestures harmonize
he's made a new friend

yes, he's alienated

from the mainstream

yet he has found himself

THE FATE OF A BRILLIANT YOUNG MIND

In her country, Iran, she's revered by both
children and adults as a national treasure
she's just seven years old,
has a very pretty face and wears a silk scarf
she attends a private school
where the study of the Koran
comes before all other subjects
Anywhere else in the world
she would be considered a little genius
not only does she dress neatly
and comports herself like a young lady
but she has an astounding memory
Her language is Persian, or Farsi
yet she knows the Koran by heart
which is written in Arabic, all 600 + pages,
without understanding a word of it,
except for Allah and Mohammed
and the names of Islam's holy places
She's become so famous
that she's been invited to make sermons
at the country's main mosques
in the men's only space

You ought to see with what fervor
they listen to her, drinking every syllable,
like an elixir concocted by the angels,
warning them of God's terrible vengeance
should anyone of them follow the wrong path
the words punishment, maimings and death
flow from her sweet lips like so many rose petals
and lo and behold, you ought to see
how these adults start crying, some
almost reaching a state of trance
don't we hear what a crime it is
to waste a young child's mind?
Once that little girl reaches the age
of puberty, she won't be allowed
to enter the men's space at the mosque
for the moment she gets her menses
she won't be considered pure anymore
poor little girl whose fame will soon wane
poor little girl who will have to join all of us
sinners, apostates and infidels

MISSED APPOINTMENT

Could you tell me where ...
I dunno ... so you dunno
then hoo hoo the hell nose?

at the last minute
my partner couldn't make it
and I'll be alone

Music-hall de Paris
a cosy bistro, dim lights
a place for romance

grand ivory piano
trombone, violin and strings
the voice of a nightingale

a Brasilian tune
just for those two lovers
huddled behind their table

the wheel of life turns

then suddenly
the keynotes roll on
in a frenzy

the temperature rises
inside my arteries
rebellion seethes

solitude has left me
a well of emotions
fills my every pore

I'm suffocating
there's war around my heart
what am I doing here?

I get up in a whiff
a glass breaks in smithereens
and my world falls apart

IN THE GARDENS OF VILLA BORGHESE

the air is cracking
with thunder and zipping clouds
rush of butterflies

the woods are graced with
the statues of foreign poets
abode of lizards

around Pushkin
a Roman family
sets a picnic table

from his pedestal
the author of 'Les Misérables'
stares at a kissing couple

the New York massacres
continue to rent my heart
as a swan beckons to me

on the islet of
the laghetto, the rustling of
a weeping willow

so much beauty
amid a world of hatred
and the gods rejoice

the Belgian and
Rumanian academies
the Scuola Britannica

twilight sets over
the Borghese gardens
cruising of young fauns

in this gorgeous landscape
commences the ballet of
courting automobiles

acrid smell of pine
young men masturbating
each other in the dark

THE BEAUTY OF SYMMETRY

Maybe there is a biological explanation
maybe it is just an aesthetic rule
that God or whosoever has created
the animal kingdom decided that
we should all be that way
I cannot believe it is the result
of a sheer accident
Why do we have two eyes
separated by a nose
two arms and two legs
in perfect symmetry
When our innards are set
at random, or so it appears?
It's as if that deity or Nature
wanted to hide the functions of life
the way we do when we build a car
concealing its motor under a hood
and making sure
the outer body
is as pleasing to the eye
Look at the ugliest of reptilians
and you will find that common trait
What would we have looked like
if we just had a transparent
envelope covering our entrails?
Would we still be beautiful?

Street art, Tel Aviv, Israel

Albert Russo who has published worldwide over 75 books of poetry, fiction and photography, in both English and French, is the recipient of many awards, such as The New York Poetry Forum and Amelia (CA) awards, The American Society of Writers Fiction Award, The British Diversity Short Story Award and the Prix Colette, among others. His work has been translated into a dozen languages in 25 countries, on the five continents. He has garnered several prizes for his photography books, Indie Excellence awards, among others. Some of his photos have been exhibited at the prestigious Museum of Photography in Lausanne, Switzerland. He was also a member of the 1996 jury for the Neustadt International Prize for Literature which often leads to the Nobel Prize of Literature.

Praising the poet and the writer

«Dear Albert Russo:

I've read everything you sent me, and I like your work very much indeed. It has a very gentle surface and a savage under-tow and I applaud the wicked portrait of Ionesco.»
　　　　　All the best, JAMES BALDWIN

DOUGLAS PARMEE, Poet and translator (Queens' College, University of Cambridge, UK):
"... I was particularly impressed by the remarkable range shown in such a small space, and the extraordinary command of the language. Albert Russo will one day produce an important body of work."

PIERRE EMMANUEL , Poet (Académie Française):
"... I want to tell you the pleasure I had upon reading those difficult, sensuous pages ... yet full of humor."

PAUL WILLEMS, Curator of the Brussels Museum of Fine Arts and Author: "From the onset I felt a new tone in Albert Russo's work, to which one cannot remain indifferent."

JOSEPH KESSEL (Author of *The Lion* and *The Horsemen*, both made into films, and world reporter - Académie Française):
"... I was very touched by the tone of your two books."

Lake of Galilee, Israel

EMBERS UNDER MY SKIN - Poems and Photos by Albert Russo

About Albert Russo's CROWDED WORLD OF SOLITUDE, vol.2, (547 pages),
a book of poems encompassing 30 years of writing. Excerpts of reviews

David Alexander in *Taj Mahal Review* (India)

    It also seems to me that the poet often needs to be considered as much as the poem. Albert Russo, who lives in Paris not far from the Place de la Concorde, is situated at an excellent geographical and psychic crossroads to appreciate what can happen when society is at war with itself. Russo, who was born in Africa of Sephardic and Italian stock, attended school in Brooklyn, and has lived in Paris for much of the last three decades, began writing in English and has wound up composing in both English and his adopted French with equal verve. As might well befit someone as quintessentially polyglot as he, Russo is also inveterately footloose. He rarely stays put for long. His globetrotting has paid off in fresh insights that you can't get from watching the news on television.
    Like all poetry, Russo's work chronicles his inner life and his outer existence in society, but unlike many other poets' works, Russo has a gift for making statements of simple clarity in a few lines that might well be prose and not poetry but for the fact that in their fine distillation of nuances of meaning they embody the essence of the poetic. This may explain the many haikus, or faux haikus (for many of them are far longer than conventional haikus) and haiku sequences, found in the collection.

JoSelle Vanderhooft in *The Pedestal Magazine* (USA)

Multilingual poet and novelist Albert Russo´s most recent poetry collection, The Crowded World of Solitude, Volume II (which followed the first volume´s issue by a matter of months) is one of that rarest of books, one which seems to contain a hearty cross-section of the writer´s output over the past several years. Frequently its themes are just as ambitious as its size; in the book´s more than five hundred pages, Russo writes on such eternal subjects as the vicissitudes of love, the impersonality of modern living, and man´s inhumanity toward man. He also tackles smaller, more immediate subjects, including Aesop-like animal fables, odes to female beauty, even complaints about the unfairness of publishers and literary critics. Merely seen as a retrospective of an artist´s output, the collection is as interesting as it is unusual, as the work of most contemporary poets is not typically available in such a large volume.

View from the Trocadéro, Paris, France

EMBERS UNDER MY SKIN - Poems and Photos by Albert Russo

La Nef des Fous (France)

Whether through his novels, his short stories or his poems, Albert Russo approaches humankind in all its complexity; man's doubts, his anguishes, his pleasures: nothing escapes the artist's scrutiny.

His poetry is resolutely modern, even when it is anchored in history. His main concern is to delve into the anima in its globablity, i.e., studying the human being, both as an individual and in his environment. He never falls into the trap of pomposity when tackling man as a social being or becomes maudlin, when considered in his uniqueness. He is neither an ideologue nor an egocentric, which is often the case with second rate poets.

His poetry is original in that it almost always tells a story. Indeed, Albert Russo uses the narrative medium whilst at the same time the poem remains introspective. For above all, he's a story teller, and the poem, in his hands, becomes a tale, a fable, a slice of life. Let me clarify things: it is of genuine verse that I am speaking, and not of some piece of writing disguised as poetry, for Albert Russo excels in the various genres he tackles, and he allows no confusion, even if at times, he plays around with them introducing poetry into a novel.

The style is free, sharp, pugnacious, it can also be caustic and humorous, or plainly humane. The story, no matter how brief, is always precise and full of empathy. Never gratuitous, it breathes life into the subject or the anecdote, yet never being anecdotal. He delves deeply into the human sould, even when the them appears in its lightness or its futility. The language - or rather, languages, since many of his poems are bilingual (in English and in French, with forays into Italian, Spanish and German - he uses is beautifully crafted and elegant, which doesn't mean that he avoids neologisms or even slang. This is what I call mastery.

Reach Magazine (UK)

Make no mistake, this is a BIG book. A full 540 pages of Albert Russo' s collected poems, including a bilingual section. A long-time Reach subscriber, Russo speaks 5 languages fluently and has lived on 3 continents. He writes in both Eng1ish and French, bis two 'mother tangues'. The confines and priorities of Reach mean that a full review just isn't possible here, but this is a collection of the finest contemporary poetry. I like reviews that stand alone wim the poet's words, and his wide experience means that there is a 'roundness' to this volume as a whole. He doesn't shy away from any subject but enters with utter enthusiasm as readers may have noticed from his published work in this and other magazines.

EMBERS UNDER MY SKIN - Poems and Photos by Albert Russo 125

Modern Metro entrance, Paris, France

EMBERS UNDER MY SKIN - Poems and Photos by Albert Russo

Adam Donaldson Powell, Norwegian-American poet and artist:

In an age where blatant shows of superiority are often considered a provocation, Albert Russo presents the ailing world of literary criticism with several challenges of mammoth proportions. His mastery of several literary genres, his indefatigable literary output, his command of several languages, his intellectual breadth, and the scope of his cultural and sub-cultural personal life experiences alone outclass the qualifications and/or capacities of many literary critics of this century.

Albert Russo is truly on the fast-track to becoming "famous" in his own lifetime, and indeed shows much courage and self-confidence in publishing such a formidable and challenging volume of collected poems non-posthumously. Perhaps even more so considering that poetry is not his only genre of acclaim. We live in an era where informed (and uninformed) critics often insist upon categorizing artists and artistic genius within a specific discipline, genre or art form; and where he/she who attempts to be too multidisciplinary is often considered to be "lightweight" or a "jack-of-all-trades". Albert Russo is an exception to all of the abovementioned society-imposed and self-imposed restrictions, and clearly recalls a multidisciplinary usage of talent more particular to previous eras.

To publish one's collected poems to-date in such a large volume, spanning some thirty years of life experiences and literary development, is a very bold statement in itself. Such a collection of poems – like any other serious literary work – is expected to be even in quality, hopefully diverse in content and form, and appropriately polished (the degree of polish being both intentional and commensurate with the desired expression). In addition, writing a bilingual volume of collected poems further adds to the complexities of such an endeavour, giving rise to many questions and solutions regarding choice of original language versus translation, idiom, culture, visual communication etc.

Mr. Russo does not disappoint, and he does – in fact – both deliver substance, and an undaunted and relentless display of consistency in terms of excellent insight and craftsmanship. His collection of poetry, at times biting and hard-hitting, is both thought-provoking, amusing, intelligent and contemporary in style and subject matter.

This collection of poems denotes a clear and masterful demonstration of quality, breadth of content and form, political and social awareness, mastery of storytelling, a touch of the "bad boy", a combination of the highly-polished and the "intentionally-raw", and visual, musical and philosophical expressions indicative of the author's rich multicultural and experiential personal history. I find in his poetry the same literary achievements which characterize his novels and short stories: balance of intellectual rationalism and emotional presence, a solid command of the full palette of language(s) used, descriptive colour, clarity, intentional usage of abstractions, entertainment and theatrical/performance value, humour and occasional irony, and an overall sense of when to use poetic economy versus poetic rapture. Mr. Russo's poetry proclaims an almost haunting sense of musicality and visual portrayal on a subjective level. Most importantly, I find that his poetry has the power of arousing within the reader a sense of personal identification, emotion and engagement – evoking a pas de deux between author and reader, all the while challenging the "poet" in the reader.

The Seine in Paris, France

Preface by LEIGH EDUARDO, British poet and musician.

I have never met Albert Russo and yet, through his writing, I feel I have had that privilege. He possesses that rare and enviable talent of being able to say what is important in a very few words. His contributions to the literary world are amazingly varied, reminding one of an intellectual butterfly - able to flit from one topic to another, but having first drained it of its essential qualities.

Russo writes at all levels - a compulsive creator who is always going to have something important, or *different* , or both, to say. He tackles any subject matter with the same enthusiasm by which his work suggests he lives. Certainly, he can never be considered squeamish!

Russo's latest work is proof of this. It's a collection which reaches into the very soul of contemporary living. While the images are well-observed, they are essentially poetic, satisfying even the most literary's heart lust for colourful verbal epitomising. Here, one comes to grips with many contemporary problems, all beautifully crafted and possessing the Russo hallmark of subtle observation.

It's usual in a collection for one or two pieces to stand out above the rest, rather like landmarks on a lovely scene. Russo's variation and treatment of so many issues makes such selectivity impossible; each poem is a gem in its own right.

Parisian fashion in the 1950's

EMBERS UNDER MY SKIN - Poems and Photos by Albert Russo

General introduction to Albert Russo's work by Martin Tucker,
poet, editor in chief of Confrontation magazine and biographer of Joseph Conrad and Sam Shepard, among other writers:

Albert Russo's art and life are all of a unique piece, and that piece is a plurality of cultures. Born in what was then the Belgian Congo and now is Congo/Zaire, he grew up in Central and Southern Africa and writes in both English and French, his two 'mother tongues'. With his intense interest in African life, the young Russo also engaged with knowledge beyond narrow stratifications of colonial custom. As a youth he left Africa for college in New York (where he attended New York University). For many years he has been resident in Paris. Wherever he has lived, Russo has concerned himself with one hard-burning commitment: to achieve an illumination of vision in his writing that suggests by the force of its light some direction for understanding of human behavior and action. He draws on the many cultures he has been privileged to know, and he is always respectul of diversity. But Russo is no mere reporter. While he works with words, and while his work is concerned with place and the spirit of place, he is more interested in visitation than visits. Almost every fiction Russo has written involves a visitation, a hearing from another world that reverberates into a dénouement and revolution of the protagonist's present condition. These visitations are of course a form of fabulism--that is, utilizing the fable as a subtext of the animal nature of man. Russo's fabulism however is not in the line of traditional mythology (perhaps mythologies is a better term, since Russo draws from a variety of folklore and consummate literary executions). In one of his recent fictions, for example, he writes of a man who falls in love with a tree--his love is so ardent he wills himself into a tree in order to root out any foreignness in his love affair. Thus, Russo's "family tree", the mating of woodland Adam and Eve, becomes in his creation not only a multicultural act but a cross-fertilization of the cultures he has drawn from. In this personal fable Russo suggests the Greek myth of Pan love and even the Adamastor legend, that Titan who has turned cruelly into a rock out of unbridled passion for a goddess. Russo suggests other legends as well, and certainly the crossing of boundaries, psychological, emotional as well as physical and territorial--hybrid phenomena now sweeping into the attention of all of Africa and the Middle East--is to be found within the feelingful contours of his tale.
Fabulism is now a recognized presence in our literary lives. It goes by other names: magic realism is one of them. Underneath all the manifestations of this phenomenon is the artistic credo that creation is larger than life, and that the progeny created enhances the life that gave being to it. In sum, the artist is saying that life is larger than life if given the opportunity to be lived magnificently. Russo's is certainly a part of this willingness to experiment beyond the observable. His fiction represents, in essence, a belief, in the endless perceivable possibilities of mind. Its humor is at times dark, however, and perhaps this color of mood is a reflection of Russo's background and biography. For his art, while enlarging, is not showered with sun. His dark hues are those of ironic vision.

Russo may be said to be very much a part of the end of this century. His concentration is on the inevitabilities of unknowingness; thus his resort is to the superrational as a way of steadying himself in the darkness. At the same time his work cannot be said to be tragic, for the unending endings of his fictions suggest a chance of progress, if not completion of one's appointed task, worlds meet and become larger worlds in Russo's work; people change within his hands. It is a pleasure to pay homage to Russo's achievement.

www.ingramcontent.com/pod-product-compliance
Lightning Source LLC
Chambersburg PA
CBHW041616220426
43671CB00001B/8